· · · · · · · ✦ · · · · · · ·

A GIFT FOR *Jen & Jena*

FROM *Loewp Grandparents*

DATE *12-23-2022*

The Gift of Jesus

MEDITATIONS FOR CHRISTMAS

CHARLES F. STANLEY

THOMAS NELSON
Since 1798

ISBN 978-1-4002-3888-0 (audiobook)
ISBN 978-1-4002-3887-3 (eBook)
ISBN 978-1-4002-3886-6 (HC)

Printed in China

22 23 24 25 26 GRI 10 9 8 7 6 5 4 3 2 1

Contents

REGAINING THE SIGNIFICANCE OF CHRISTMAS

⁎

*You will seek Me and find Me when you
search for Me with all your heart.*

JEREMIAH 29:13

In the midst of all your holiday preparations and festivities, do you take time to read the Christmas story? Is it still as beautiful and meaningful as it was when you first came to know Jesus as your Savior? Or do you skim the verses, thinking, *I know this account so well. The lack of rooms at the inn, the manger, the angels, the shepherds—I don't really need to go over it all again.* Sadly, for many, the familiarity of the story means that what happened on that awesome night has lost its significance and power in their lives.

This is why I have written this book, reflecting on the greatest gift God has ever given: Himself. I pray that rather than skipping the biblical account, you will make it the centerpiece of your celebration and allow it to speak into your life. This is my habit as Christmas approaches each December—I meditate on the history-changing day when God "became flesh, and dwelt among us" (John 1:14). I think about the birth of Christ and consider all that it means to the world and to me personally. Though I've studied the Christmas story year after year, I never want it to grow stale. Rather, I desire for the reality of "God with us" (Matthew 1:23 NLT) to remain real and fresh in my mind and circumstances. I long for the humility of our Savior and the glory of His eternal plan to pierce my heart as it did the first time I read it.

And every year, the Father reveals something new and wonderful about what He accomplished at Christ's birth. For example, one year He showed me the awesome wisdom and simplicity of the name *Jesus*. Any child can say it. But imagine if the Messiah's name had been Bartholomew, Zephaniah, Habakkuk, or Zechariah? That would have been far too difficult for the little ones to pronounce.

I recall that when she was a small child, my sister could not say the word *brother*, so she always called me "Bubby." That was the only way she could address me at that early age. But she could certainly say "Jesus." She could declare the sweetest name on earth—the name that literally means "God's deliverer." When the Father showed me that in Scripture, it strengthened my faith in His astounding wisdom and loving provision.

The truth of the matter is this: Christmas can be a difficult time of year and can pass us by in a blur. This is why I think we can do nothing better than take a long, profound look at the account. We need an intimate look at the birth of Jesus. It can only benefit us to ask, "What does God have to say to me about all this right now?"

So as you read this book and all the passages of Scripture that speak to the Christmas story, realize that the Father *wants* to reveal Himself to you in a personal way. It makes a tremendous difference in your Bible reading when you realize that God has a message He wants you to receive. You are not simply learning facts or being entertained with a story. You are interacting with your living Savior, who "emptied Himself, taking the form of a bond-servant" (Philippians 2:7) so you can have a relationship with Him. This is what the Christmas story is all about. God

Jesus is the sweetest name on earth—the name that literally means "God's deliverer."

desires for you to experience His presence, obtain comfort in His grace, and find direction for your daily life. If you examine Scripture and read these reflections with the anticipation of hearing Him, you'll be amazed at what He will show you.

Therefore, ask God to teach you how to apply what you read to your circumstances. Simply pray, "Father, what are You saying to me? How does this account relate to my life, and how should I proceed with what You reveal to me?" You may wonder, *The birth of Christ was more than two thousand years ago—how can it possibly relate to me today?* Be assured, He wants to show you. In fact, He promises, "Call to Me and I will answer you, and I will tell you great and mighty things, which you do not know" (Jeremiah 33:3).

I would also encourage you to trust God and submit to Him, regardless of what He tells you to do. The Lord does not require you to understand His will, just obey it, even if it seems unreasonable. At the time, it may not have made much sense that our Savior was born of a virgin in a rough stable in Bethlehem, but we know it was His perfect plan for our salvation. Learn from the faith Mary and Joseph demonstrated and trust the Father however He may lead you.

As I said, I hope that rather than skipping the biblical account of the birth of Jesus, you will make it the centerpiece of your celebration this Christmas and meditate on the history-changing day when our Savior came to dwell among us. Surely, spending time with God is always the very best present you can give yourself. May the Lord bless you as you focus on Him, and may you have a very Merry Christmas.

CHAPTER ONE

A JOURNEY OF LOVE

* * * * * * ✦ * * * * * *

*God showed how much he loved us by sending
his one and only Son into the world so that
we might have eternal life through him.*

1 JOHN 4:9 NLT

On December 17, 1903, near Kitty Hawk, North Carolina, Orville and Wilbur Wright were the first people in history to successfully take flight. Their first attempt lasted only twelve seconds, but in those fleeting moments and the ones that followed, they changed the course of how humanity would travel.

Then on July 20, 1969, astronauts Neil Armstrong and Edwin "Buzz" Aldrin became the first humans ever to land and walk on the moon. Although the Apollo 11 mission lasted only eight days, the subsequent advances in science, technology, and medicine that proceeded from the space program would also impact civilization in astounding ways.

While these have been noteworthy events, there is another journey that covered more miles and made a greater impact on the world than any other in all of history. And it not only has the power to transform every moment of every day but also to change your eternity.

Of course, I am talking about the birth of Christ. And the more you and I recognize what transpired when Jesus left His throne in heaven, the better we will understand how much God loves us and the lengths He went to in order to help us. You see, Jesus did not take on His mission out of a sense of adventure or for the technological advancement of civilization. Rather, He did so because He genuinely loves us. Christ sincerely wants to redeem us, heal us, and fill up all the places in our lives that are lacking. This is important for you and me to appreciate because when we grasp how profoundly the Lord truly cares for us, we will be more motivated to draw near to Him in a close, personal relationship. And the more intimate our fellowship with Him, the more meaning, fulfillment, and contentment we are going to enjoy in our Christian life, even when things aren't how we envisioned they would be.

I write this because—especially at Christmastime—you may be worn out by trying to figure things out. Maybe you are a new believer and you're not quite sure what this season is all about. Or perhaps you've been a Christian for a long time, and the joy seems to have faded. It could even be that life has discouraged you, loneliness has overwhelmed you, others have disappointed you, or you don't see much of a future ahead. You love Jesus, but the Christian life sometimes feels unfulfilling or even draining.

This is why it is so important to reflect on God's greatest gift to us—the gift of Himself. You see, I think at times the reason we grow weary and hopeless is because we're so focused on our circumstances that we've forgotten to fix our eyes on Jesus Himself. We need more than a quick quiet time; rather, our souls yearn to experience His presence and worship Him in the fullness of who He is.

Therefore, we must begin at the right starting point when we think about this journey of love called *Christmas*—though it is not, as many imagine, in the manger at Bethlehem. Rather, about Jesus, John 1:1 tells us, "In the beginning was the Word, and the Word was with God, and the Word was God." Before the foundation of the world, Jesus existed and was actively involved

*

Our souls yearn

to experience

Jesus' presence.

in the creation of all things because He is God. He set the sun, moon, and stars in their places; divided the heavens from the earth and land from the waters; created all living things—every genus of plant and animal—and breathed life into Adam and Eve. He is the eyewitness of all history, the miracle-working deliverer of Israel, and the One who sustains everything from the smallest subatomic particles to the vast workings of the universe.

Before Jesus ever appeared on the scene as a baby in Bethlehem, He stood in the place of honor—at the right hand of the throne of heaven (Psalm 110:1; Mark 16:19). Yet, Philippians 2:5–7 goes on to say, "Christ Jesus, who, although He existed in the form of God, did not regard equality with God a thing to be grasped, but emptied Himself, taking the form of a bond-servant, and being made in the likeness of men."

We may be able to measure the distances the Wright brothers flew, or Armstrong and Aldrin traversed, and consider all they were risking to advance science and technology. However, we would be hard-pressed to quantify the vast and incalculable expanse between the throne of God and wherever we are here on earth and also the sacrifice it took for Jesus to give up one for the other. Our minds might not fully comprehend the distances He crossed in relation to light-years or miles—certainly human measurements would scarcely suffice. But what is genuinely important is for us to contemplate how far Christ came from His glory in heaven.

We see a picture of the majesty and honor the Lord receives

in Daniel 7, where we are told God's throne is ablaze with flames, and thousands upon thousands attend Him (vv. 9–10). Daniel recounted the awesome scene:

> With the clouds of heaven One like a Son of Man was coming, and He came up to the Ancient of Days and was presented before Him. And to Him was given dominion, glory and a kingdom, that all the peoples, nations and men of every language might serve Him. His dominion is an everlasting dominion which will not pass away; and His kingdom is one which will not be destroyed. (vv. 13–14)

Then, in Revelation 4, with Jesus at the place of honor on the right hand and the Holy Spirit before the throne, we are told the Godhead receives praise continually:

> Four living creatures, each one of them having six wings . . . day and night they do not cease to say, "Holy, holy, holy is the Lord God, the Almighty, who was and who is and who is to come."
>
> And when the living creatures give glory and honor and thanks to Him who sits on the throne, to Him who lives forever and ever, the twenty-four elders will fall down before Him who sits on the throne, and will worship Him who lives forever and ever, and will cast their crowns before the throne, saying, "Worthy are You, our Lord and our God, to receive

What is genuinely important
is for us to contemplate
how far Christ came from
His glory in heaven.

glory and honor and power; for You created all things, and because of Your will they existed, and were created." (vv. 8–11)

Imagine being the eternal, unmatched, and rightful King, and having complete command of the universe, as well as all creation as your footstool. Would there be anything that could make you give all that up? Yet, Jesus did not hesitate. He did not send someone else. And He did not take shortcuts in the hopes of avoiding pain. Jesus left heaven where He was so highly revered, where He resided in the pinnacle of glory and majesty, and where He was attended by the hosts of angels, to suffer as a humble and lowly servant because that is what it took for Him to save you. And He did it because of how profoundly He loves you.

It may be beyond comprehension that the exalted Sovereign of heaven and earth would give Himself for you in such a sacrificial manner. But this was how Christ's journey of love began. The Lord of the universe came to be your gift—emptying Himself so that He could identify with you completely and understand your struggles from the inside out.

So today you may be hurting from sacrifices you've made, disappointments you've endured, and losses you've sustained. You may be wondering if anyone notices how you struggle. Does anyone even see you? Be assured, Jesus cares deeply about your pain, your disheartenment, and even your feelings of helplessness. In fact, Christmas is proof that He has traversed every dimension and distance and made every sacrifice necessary to prove beyond a shadow of doubt that He "is near to the brokenhearted and saves those who are crushed in spirit" (Psalm 34:18). The journey that brought Him to you was fueled by His love. And as you will see in the following pages, absolutely nothing can stop Him from being with you every step of the way (Romans 8:38–39).

A Moment of Reflection

Have you ever taken a journey—especially a very difficult one—out of love for another person? What kinds of sacrifices did you have to make? What made the trip worthwhile to you? Write your thoughts below.

How did the person react to your sacrifices? How did the way they responded make you feel?

_____

_____

_____

_____

_____

_____

Compare your experience to what Jesus left behind to come to earth. Spend some time thanking Him for each thing you can think of that He gave up or had to face for you.

_____

_____

_____

_____

_____

_____

_____

A Gift for Today

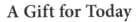

God's activity in your life and interactions with you are motivated by His holy and unconditional love.

Of the Father's Love begotten
Ere the worlds began to be,
He is Alpha and Omega,
He the source, the ending He,
Of the things that are, that have been,
And that future years shall see,
Evermore and evermore.
This is He Whom seers in old time
Chanted of with one accord;
Whom the voices of the Prophets
Promised in their faithful word;
Now He shines, the long-expected;
Let creation praise its Lord:
Evermore and evermore!
O ye heights of heaven adore Him!
Angel-hosts His praises sing!
All dominions bow before Him,
And extol our God and King;
Let no tongue on earth be silent,
Every voice in concert ring,
Evermore and evermore!

"OF THE FATHER'S LOVE BEGOTTEN" BY
AURELIUS CLEMENS PRUDENTIUS[1]

CHAPTER TWO

JESUS: GOD IN THE FLESH

· · · · · · · ✦ · · · · · · ·

The Word became flesh, and dwelt
among us, and we saw His glory,
glory as of the only begotten from the
Father, full of grace and truth.

JOHN 1:14

It is not usually an easy transition to go from thinking God is a distant, supreme being to realizing that in Jesus, the world has seen and interacted with the Lord of all creation. I have found that whenever I talk about the divinity of Christ, people have questions about what I mean. I recall being seated at a luncheon one day and a lady said, "For over sixty years I went to church, and I heard about Jesus. I thought I knew about Him. Until one Sunday when I turned on the *In Touch* program. All of a sudden, I realized I didn't really know who He was at all. Is Jesus really God?"

Of course, the fact that Jesus Christ is God is the foundational truth we celebrate at Christmas: the incarnation of the Lord God Almighty becoming flesh in the Person of Jesus in that stable in Bethlehem. Yet, it is understandable that people have trouble reconciling the fact that Jesus is fully divine while also being completely human. After all, the manner by which the Lord is presented to us in the Old Testament is awesome for sure—He is the eternal, everlasting, almighty, living God; the Great I Am; the Most High Sovereign of all that exists, who is absolutely holy, infinite in power, and unfailingly faithful. We often learn about Him in the Old Testament by His Hebrew names, *Elohim, Adonai, El Shaddai,* and *Yahweh Yireh*—titles that are beautiful and powerful, but somewhat distant and mysterious to us. Yet Jesus is so kind, loving, and approachable. He is the Good Shepherd, the Great Physician, and the Lamb of God. Whenever we read about Him interacting with others, He is so relatable, down to earth, and compassionate—always sacrificially willing to teach, heal, and redeem.

The obvious question is how can Jesus and the Father both be God when we understand them as distinct? How can the powerful hands that forcefully carved the mountains and canyons be the same that gently touched the eyes of the blind man to restore his sight? Scripture reveals that the Almighty is Trinity—one God, yet three Persons: the Father, the Son, and the Holy Spirit. We use the term *persons* because each has a unique role and expression in the Godhead. Though the three Persons of the Trinity are all fully God, they are not three deities. Rather, together they are one God, operating in perfect union and communion in one essence.

It is true Jesus was completely human, but the wonderful, supernatural mystery is that He was also wholly divine. Believing this is absolutely essential for your faith. He is both the One who set the holy standard for salvation and the One who fulfills it on our behalf. And Jesus does this because as fully God and fully man, He is the only One who can.

But what we need to understand is that Jesus came to reveal the true nature of God the Father to humanity. Jesus is the radiance of His glory, the exact representation of His nature. In other words Jesus shows us what it looks like when our divine, all-powerful, incomprehensibly awesome God interacts with us on a personal level. Christ said it Himself: "He who has seen Me has seen the Father" (John 14:9). When you look at who Jesus is throughout Scripture, you are observing that the Lord is a God of mercy,

How can the powerful hands that
forcefully carved the mountains
be the same that gently touched
the eyes of the blind man?

loving-kindness, holiness, justice, wisdom, redemption, healing, and power in bodily form. And when you know who He truly is, you understand why He is worthy of all honor, glory, and praise.

Some people say they're Christians but don't acknowledge the divinity of Christ. They think He was simply a good teacher, philosopher, social reformer, or healer. I want to be crystal clear on this matter: you can believe all of these wonderful things about Jesus, but if you do not accept that Jesus Christ is God the Son and that He is the only One who can save you from your sins, then you do not actually know Him.

The Jesus who reached out to others in Scripture is the same God in heaven who calls to you, offering love, redemption, wisdom, guidance, and healing no matter what you've done or what you face. Therefore, take time today to appreciate Him for who He really is.

A Moment of Reflection

Look up and write out what we learn about Jesus in the following verses:

Hebrews 1:1–3:

_____

_____

_____

Colossians 1:15–20:

How does understanding who Jesus is impact what you are facing today? Is there anything He cannot handle?

Spend time praising God for who He is.

A Gift for Today

The kind, loving, and approachable Jesus is the all-powerful, all-knowing, ever-present God—and He is always willing to help you, guide you, teach you, heal you, and redeem you.

Christ, by highest heav'n adored,
Christ, the everlasting Lord:
Late in time behold Him come,
Offspring of a virgin's womb.
Veiled in flesh the Godhead see,
Hail th' incarnate Deity!
Pleased as man with man to dwell,
Jesus our Immanuel.
Hark! the herald angels sing,
"Glory to the new-born King!"
"HARK! THE HERALD ANGELS SING" ORIGINAL
LYRICS BY CHARLES WESLEY[2]

CHAPTER THREE

PREPARATION FOR THE JOURNEY

· · · · · · ✦ · · · · · ·

When the fullness of the time came,
God sent forth His Son.

GALATIANS 4:4

Have you ever arranged to take a long trip far from home? If you have, you know all the details that must be put in order so that the journey can be a success. As you can imagine, when Christ traversed the great expanse between heaven and earth and put on human flesh, a great deal of preparation was involved. The Lord wanted every provision to be perfectly in place when He revealed His plan of salvation to us.

However, if I were to ask what kind of groundwork God laid for the coming of His Son, most people might think in terms of Mary and Joseph traveling from Nazareth to Bethlehem or about some of the other events of that extraordinary night. But when Paul wrote about "the fullness of the time" (Galatians 4:4), he understood the infinite preparation the Lord had made in arranging for this special moment we call Christmas. Paul realized that from ancient times, God's great providential hand had orchestrated the events that would ultimately change the course of human history and the eternal destinations of all who would believe in Jesus. Indeed, God even arranged the stars in the sky to testify about Christ's incarnation.

You see, from the fall of Adam and Eve in the garden of Eden—which set into motion our need for a Savior—to the night of Christ's birth, God has been working towards our redemption, despite our continued rebellion against Him. The plan took more than two thousand years, but slowly and surely, He prepared the way. Reaching down into the pagan society of Ur, God chose Abraham to be the father of the Israelite people, through

God's great providential hand
had orchestrated the events
that would ultimately change
the course of human history.

whom the Messiah would come. Eventually the Israelites would end up as slaves in Egypt, so the Lord raised up Moses to lead His chosen people out of bondage and into the land they would call their own. God also gave the nation of Israel the Mosaic law by which all people were to live. Through the Law, humanity would discover that "there is no one who does good" (Psalm 14:1). We all fail to reach God's holy requirements and have no way to save ourselves.

Yet the Lord, through His prophets, gave us hope—promising at many times and in various ways that He was coming and that He would provide a way for us to be forgiven of our sins and know Him. He gave these prophesies in a way that we would know exactly who the Messiah would be by identifying His nationality, His family line, the place of His birth, and even the time when the Savior would be born. We will see the awesome and meticulous ways Jesus fulfilled these promises in the pages ahead.

However, what is important for us to understand is that while God was overseeing His chosen people through whom He would send the world a Savior, He was also governing the affairs of the nations surrounding them. In fact, six great empires were involved in His plan, and as you read the histories of how Israel interacted with Egypt, Assyria, Babylon, Medo-Persia, Greece, and Rome, you can see the guiding hand of the Lord working to provide a Redeemer who would save people from their sins. You see, through these nations, God prepared a unified language so all people could understand His message, safe roads for missionaries to travel and spread the good news, synagogues as outposts for the proclamation of the gospel, and a postal system through which letters to the churches could be sent. He even had His people gather a canon of Scripture so they could demonstrate that what God had promised had been fulfilled.

It may appear to the casual reader that nations and rulers—both good and evil—have guided human history. That is how most things will appear from our vantage point—we see only what our limited human sight can behold. But it is not so. God would not leave His great purposes for humanity in the weak and unpredictable hands of people. Rather, He has always been in control. Almighty God, in eternity past, meticulously protected every single prophecy, moved men, nations, civilizations, and even the heavens to prepare the world for the mission of His only begotten Son, Jesus. When the Lord is involved, everything goes to plan in perfect order.

Of course, you may think, *It certainly took God a long time to carry all that out.* And perhaps there is something in your life that is taking longer than you think it should. Maybe plans you've had have gone awry or you find yourself in an odd position, questioning what the future holds. But remember, the Lord's schedule is not our own. He is in the process of doing something infinitely bigger than you and I could possibly conceive. And for us to have hope, we must trust that God is in sovereign control of all creation and that He works meticulously to fulfill every promise.

Therefore, do not lose heart. You are in the preparation stage,

✳

God moved men, nations,
civilizations, and even the heavens
to prepare the world for the mission
of His only begotten Son, Jesus.

and the Lord is moving all the puzzle pieces into place. And when the fullness of time comes for you, God's plan will be beyond what you can ask or imagine. He has not faltered throughout the history of the world, and He will not fail you now.

A Moment of Reflection

Have you had any delays or interruptions in your plans lately? Think about all the incidents that hindered what you wanted to accomplish and write them below—even the smallest detail you can think of that caused your schedule to derail.

In the story of Christmas, we see that nothing on earth can prevent God from carrying out His plans. Daniel 2:21 affirms, "He controls the course of world events; he removes kings and sets up other kings" (NLT). With this in mind, read Romans 8:38–39 and write your thoughts about the verses below.

_____

_____

_____

_____

_____

_____

_____

Perhaps you noticed that all of the obstacles listed in Romans 8:38–39 are far beyond your ability to manage. However, they are all well within God's control. And if nothing can separate you from His love, then there is no creature, force, or circumstance in all creation that can hinder His plans for you. So spend some time praising Him for this fact today.

_____

_____

_____

_____

_____

_____

_____

A Gift for Today

God knows the plans He has for you, and He is preparing you for them. Nothing can thwart them as long as you continue walking with Him.

Draw nigh, draw nigh, O Lord of Might,
Who to Thy tribes from Sinai's height
In ancient time didst give the Law,
In cloud and majesty and awe.
Rejoice! rejoice! Emmanuel
Shall be born for thee, O Israel!
O come, Thou Wisdom from on high,
And order all things, far and nigh;
To us the path of knowledge show,
And cause us in her ways to go.
Rejoice! rejoice! Emmanuel
Shall be born for thee, O Israel!
"Veni, Veni, Emmanuel" originally in the
Psalteriolum Cantionum Catholicarum[3]

CHAPTER FOUR

A Long-Awaited Message from Heaven

. . . . ✦ . . . . . .

"He will turn many of the sons of Israel
back to the Lord their God. It is he who
will go as a forerunner before Him in the
spirit and power of Elijah . . . so as to make
ready a people prepared for the Lord."

Luke 1:16–17

When you flip through your Bible, there is a division between Malachi and Matthew—you cross from what is called the Old Testament into the New Testament. All you have to do is turn a page or two and the span is traversed between them. What we often miss, however, is that those blank pages represent four hundred years of silence from God. During that time, there were no prophesies, no updates on His activity, and no word from heaven that the Lord was still concerned about the affairs of Israel.

To put that in perspective, as I write this, the United States has been a nation almost 250 years. So God was quiet for almost double the amount of time the US has been around. And it was an eventful time for Israel. The Jews watched as ownership of their land passed from the Medo-Persians to the Greeks, and then on to the Romans. This had to have been confusing because God had promised He would return their land to them. How was it that He had handed the promised land over to three pagan superpowers and not to His own people? It was no wonder their hopes for a Messiah had faded.

But those four hundred years were like a dramatic pause before the crescendo of history. Eventually came the momentous day when a priest named Zacharias went to serve his turn in the temple. To be serving in the holy place at all was an honor that some priests never experienced because there were so many who qualified for the Levitical priesthood. But we are told, "He was chosen by lot to enter the temple of the Lord and burn incense.

And the whole multitude of the people were in prayer outside at the hour of the incense offering" (Luke 1:9–10). Zacharias's job was particularly important, because the incense symbolized the prayers of the people rising up to God. But little did he know that as the smoke from the temple sacrifices ascended to heaven, the Lord would send His messenger to answer. The angel of the Lord came to give the old priest the surprise of a lifetime, saying, "Do not be afraid, Zacharias, for your petition has been heard, and your wife Elizabeth will bear you a son, and you will give him the name John" (v. 13).

In that one moment, four hundred years of silence were broken. God was speaking to His servant Zacharias, and He was fulfilling one of the last prophesies of the Old Testament in which He declared, "Behold, I am going to send My messenger, and he will clear the way before Me. And the Lord, whom you seek, will suddenly come to His temple" (Malachi 3:1). You see, Zacharias's precious son, John, would be the forerunner to the Messiah, the hope of every Israelite (Luke 1:16–17). What made it an even greater miracle was that Zacharias and his wife, Elizabeth, were past childbearing years and had never had a child of their own.

God had not forgotten about His promises. Instead, He was working through the silent times to arrange everything necessary for the Messiah to come. But what I want you to notice here is that the faithful kept praying. They kept seeking God. They kept expecting Him to answer. And you should too. God's silences

Those four hundred years were
like a dramatic pause before
the crescendo of history.

aren't an indication that He has abandoned you. On the contrary, He works in the unseen to carry out His will.

But we need to be prepared for when He acts, and John—as the forerunner to the Savior—told us how to do so. John 1:15–18 tells us:

> John testified about [Jesus] and cried out, saying, "This was He of whom I said, 'He who comes after me has a higher rank than I, for He existed before me.'" For of His fullness we have all received, and grace upon grace. For the Law was given through Moses; grace and truth were realized through Jesus Christ. No one has seen God at any time; the only begotten God who is in the bosom of the Father, He has explained Him.

Let's break that down:

1. *"This was He of whom I said, 'He who comes after me has a higher rank than I, for He existed before me'"* (v. 15). John acknowledged that Christ has more knowledge, understanding, power, and authority than we could ever have. We must as well. Especially in the waiting times, we must recognize that God remains in charge and knows how He is leading us.
2. *"For of His fullness we have all received, and grace upon grace"* (v. 16). Like John, we must consider all the ways God has blessed us with favor, kindness, and provision. Thinking

about all the ways the Lord has helped us in the past will encourage us and help us endure the difficulties.

3. *"For the Law was given through Moses; grace and truth were realized through Jesus Christ"* (v. 17). The Law points out all the ways we fall short of God's perfect holiness. We know our faults, and often, during times when the Lord is silent, we feel especially burdened about them because we think He has rejected us. But John reminded us that grace and truth come through Jesus. Not only does Christ mercifully forgive our sins, but He teaches us how to repent—turning from our ungodly ways so we can walk in His will. Therefore, it is always good to make sure our hearts are clean before God whenever we wait for Him to answer us.

4. *"No one has seen God at any time; the only begotten God who is in the bosom of the Father, He has explained Him"* (v. 18). The best way to understand what God is doing is to look to Jesus. Study Him in Scripture. See how He interacted with others. And realize that the loving-kindness Christ demonstrated throughout Scripture is the same as He shows you—even as you wait.

When God ends the silence and shows you what He plans to accomplish, the best thing you can do is listen to what He has to say and obey Him. He does not need you to figure anything out. He already has a plan, and you must simply submit to it. Ask Him to help you listen, trust, and obey Him. The Lord is wonderfully

*

The faithful kept praying.
They kept seeking God.
They kept expecting Him to
answer. And you should too.

willing to speak to you and show you exactly what He wants to do in your life.

A Moment of Reflection

Following John's example, spend some time acknowledging that God is still in control of all that concerns you. Write your prayer to Him below.

Consider all the ways God has blessed you and provided for you in the past. Write your praises to Him below.

_____

_____

_____

_____

_____

_____

_____

_____

_____

Are there areas of your life where you are falling short of God's best for you? Is there anything you need to confess? Use the lines below to repent of your sins and agree to seek God's ways instead of your own.

_____

_____

_____

_____

_____

_____

_____

_____

_____

_____

Spend time thanking God for revealing Himself to you through Jesus, and ask Him to help you know Him better in the days and weeks to come.

_____

_____

_____

_____

_____

_____

_____

_____

_____

_____

_____

_____

_____

_____

_____

_____

_____

A Gift for Today

If the Father is quiet, then most likely there is something significant He desires to teach you, and He wants you to listen.

"Blessed be the Lord God of Israel,
For He has visited us and accomplished
redemption for His people,
And has raised up a horn of salvation for us
In the house of David His servant—
As He spoke by the mouth of His holy prophets from of old—
Salvation FROM OUR ENEMIES,
And FROM THE HAND OF ALL WHO HATE US;
To show mercy toward our fathers,
And to remember His holy covenant,
The oath which He swore to Abraham our father,
To grant us that we, being rescued from
the hand of our enemies,
Might serve Him without fear,
In holiness and righteousness before Him all our days.
And you, child, will be called the prophet of the Most High;
For you will go on BEFORE THE LORD TO PREPARE HIS WAYS;
To give to His people the knowledge of salvation
By the forgiveness of their sins,
Because of the tender mercy of our God,
With which the Sunrise from on high will visit us,
To SHINE UPON THOSE WHO SIT IN DARKNESS
AND THE SHADOW OF DEATH,
To guide our feet into the way of peace."

ZACHARIAS IN LUKE 1:68–79

CHAPTER FIVE

THE CALL OF THE FAVORED

. . . . ✦ . . . .

"Greetings, favored one! The Lord is with you."
LUKE 1:28

Whenever the Lord speaks and reveals His awesome plans, it can be both overwhelming and challenging. So it should be no surprise that the angel Gabriel's address of "Greetings, favored one! The Lord is with you" troubled Mary (Luke 1:28–29). Not only was God's messenger Gabriel likely magnificent in stature, but to hear that the Lord had singled her out for a special message must have been very astonishing to Mary, indeed. No wonder the first chapter of Luke records, "She was very perplexed at this statement, and kept pondering what kind of salutation this was" (v. 29).

However, Gabriel's message to Mary was even more astounding:

> Behold, you will conceive in your womb and bear a son, and
> you shall name Him Jesus. He will be great and will be called
> the Son of the Most High; and the Lord God will give Him
> the throne of His father David; and He will reign over the
> house of Jacob forever, and His kingdom will have no end.
> (vv. 31–33)

The familiarity of those words may desensitize us to the shock they initially caused Mary. However, read them again carefully and take a moment to think about what that announcement would sound like to a teenage girl in ancient times.

The feelings of honor must have been tremendous—she was to bear the long-awaited Messiah. It was happening! Hundreds

Hundreds of years of Israel crying out for a conquering king were finally going to be answered—and God would work through Mary to do it!

of years of Israel crying out for a conquering king were finally going to be answered—and God would work through Mary to do it! But then, the realization of the challenges involved must have been overwhelming as well. Innumerable questions must have flooded her mind, including the most obvious one: "How can this be, since I am a virgin?" (v. 34). No doubt, the fact that she would conceive through the power of the Holy Spirit would cause issues. How did that even work? She was engaged to Joseph—how would he handle the news that she was pregnant? What would people think? And how was she supposed to train this baby to be king?

One thing was certain though: Mary understood that the task set before her was far too great for her to accomplish on her own. And perhaps this is where you can relate to her. Maybe there have been times in your life when the assignments given you seemed far too difficult for you to undertake on your own, and you wondered how you would face them. You are not alone. This has been the shared experience of those who have served God throughout the ages—He often calls His people to tasks that appear impossible from the human standpoint.

We see this principle in Abraham, who was called to be the father of God's people—a nation as numerous as the stars in the sky—though he and his wife, Sarah, were barren until they were one hundred years old and ninety years old, respectively.

This pattern is also demonstrated through Moses, who—without soldiers or strategy—was charged with confronting

Pharaoh and his prodigious army in order to lead the people of Israel out of Egyptian bondage.

We observe this truth in Joshua, who was called to conquer the promised land, even though his army was made up of tired Israelites who had wandered the desert for the greater part of four decades, and the region was chock-full of Amorites, Hittites, Perizzites, Canaanites, Hivites, and Jebusites.

The assignments the Lord gives are always God-sized because His intention is to reveal Himself through them. This is why He does not choose people because of their looks, talents, intelligence, or abilities; rather, He selects people based on how much they trust Him. As we learn in 1 Samuel 16:7, "People judge by outward appearance, but the LORD looks at the heart" (NLT).

Yet one thing is sure—all who are called to serve Him have His favor. The Greek term for "favored one" that Gabriel used to address Mary means "filled with grace, highly honored, and approved by God."[4] It is found in only one other place in the New Testament—in Ephesians 1:6, where we are told that as believers, we are "accepted in the Beloved" (NKJV). Those who believe in Jesus experience God's presence in a way that is unlike anything this world has to offer. Because Christ is alive in us through His Holy Spirit, we are filled with His grace, which empowers us for all He calls us to do.

What that means is when God chooses to reveal Himself to others through you—even though He may give you a task that is far beyond your abilities—you are accepted in Him, have the

The assignments the Lord
gives are always God-sized
because His intention is to
reveal Himself through them.

honor of representing Him, and are fully equipped to do whatever He asks. And you are personally guaranteed, "Nothing will be impossible with God" (Luke 1:37).

Mary believed God, even though she could not imagine how God would accomplish all He had promised her. As with Mary, God will not tell you all the details, but He will give you enough information to proceed. And as you walk in obedience with Him, He will also encourage you, assure you that He is continually aware of your situation, and remind you that He remains sovereign.

Therefore, like Mary, demonstrate the right response for whenever God calls: "I am the Lord's servant. May everything you have said about me come true" (Luke 1:38 NLT). Then you will see His favor and know He is with you too.

A Moment of Reflection

Has God ever called you to serve Him? If so, what did He ask you to do? Write your answer below. If God has never assigned you something to do, meditate on Ephesians 2:10 and ask what good works He has prepared for you to walk in.

_____

_____

_____

_____

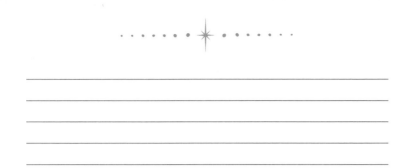

_____

_____

_____

_____

_____

Are you willing for the Lord to work through you in a powerful way? Romans 12:1 says, "I urge you, brethren, by the mercies of God, to present your bodies a living and holy sacrifice, acceptable to God, which is your spiritual service of worship." When we serve the Lord wholeheartedly, it is an act of worship because we are acknowledging who He is. Therefore, if you are willing to do whatever He may ask, present yourself to Him in prayer, offering yourself fully.

_____

_____

_____

_____

_____

A Gift for Today

You can always trust that the God who calls you will equip and empower you for whatever He gives you to do.

My soul exalts the Lord,
And my spirit has rejoiced in God my Savior.
For He has had regard for the humble state of His bondslave;
For behold, from this time on all
generations will count me blessed.
For the Mighty One has done great things for me;
And holy is His name.
AND HIS MERCY IS UPON GENERATION AFTER GENERATION
TOWARD THOSE WHO FEAR HIM.
He has done mighty deeds with His arm;
He has scattered those who were proud
in the thoughts of their heart.
He has brought down rulers from their thrones,
And has exalted those who were humble.
HE HAS FILLED THE HUNGRY WITH GOOD THINGS;
And sent away the rich empty-handed.
He has given help to Israel His servant,
In remembrance of His mercy,
As He spoke to our fathers,
To Abraham and his descendants forever.

MARY IN LUKE 1:46–55

CHAPTER SIX

HUMANITY SUPPOSES BUT GOD DISCLOSES

· · · · · · · ✦ · · · · · · ·

*In those days a decree went out from
Caesar Augustus, that a census be
taken of all the inhabited earth. . . . And
everyone was on his way to register for
the census, each to his own city.*

LUKE 2:1, 3

. . . . ✳ . . . .

Although we know the Lord is ultimately in control of history, sometimes it feels as if those in authority can do as they please. With the power they've yielded, emperors, kings, and other leaders throughout history have upended the lives of their citizens out of pride and self-interest. It presumably seemed that way for the nation of Israel. When we come to Luke 2, Rome was in control of the promised land, and the Romans were brutal, treating the Jews as though they were slaves. This was certainly the case when Caesar Augustus made a decree that everyone in the inhabited earth was required to go back to his or her city of origin for a census, most likely for the purpose of taxation.

This pronouncement, which sent many of the citizens of the Roman Empire into disarray, didn't seem like something the Lord had anything to do with. Think about it: Mary was pregnant and close to term—why would God send her on a difficult ninety-mile journey from Nazareth to Bethlehem, the city of Joseph's forefathers? One would imagine that the Lord would make those last weeks of Mary's pregnancy as safe and comfortable as possible—after all, she was carrying His Son, the Savior of the world.

It did not make sense from a human standpoint that God would not only allow but prompt this move. No doubt Caesar believed he'd made the decision on his own for his purposes as well. But from eternity past, the Lord decided who the Roman emperor would be and when he would make the historic declaration that would mean Joseph of Nazareth would take Mary to Bethlehem and ultimately give birth to Jesus there. This, of

God turned the heart of Caesar
to make a decree that would
ultimately show beyond a
shadow of a doubt that Jesus
was who He said He was—
the Promised Messiah.

course, was in fulfillment of the prophecy in Micah 5:2 that the Messiah would be born in Bethlehem, the city of King David. God turned the heart of Caesar to make a decree that would ultimately show beyond a shadow of a doubt that Jesus was who He said He was—the Promised Messiah from the line of David.

You may be wondering, *What does this have to do with me?* It has everything to do with you. At times, trouble may arise from those in authority over you, and it will be painful. You may think that the Lord cannot possibly see your pain or the wrongs being done to you. However, God may have some hidden purpose in what is happening. Joseph and Mary were right in the center of His will, but that did not prevent them from having to make that long, uncomfortable journey. Rather, the Lord worked through Caesar to move them in order to fulfill prophecy. The Father may be using those in authority over you to teach you something, help you overcome some sin, move you, or even give you a broader scope of ministry. Therefore, your smartest course of action is always to ask God in prayer to show you what you need to do.

Remember that the safest place to be is in the center of God's will, and absolutely no one can thwart His plan for you. You stay and go according to His purposes—the human authority over you is just a tool in His hand. Therefore, trust that the same God who engineered all the amazing circumstances surrounding Christ's birth in order to provide for your salvation is with you, and His ability to help you is absolutely limitless. All things concerning your life—including the hearts of people in authority over you—are in His hand. You may not be able to influence the people who could change your circumstances, but He certainly can—and He will. So take heart today that He is directing your situation like a watercourse and is helping you mightily even when it may not seem like it (Proverbs 21:1).

A Moment of Reflection

When Jesus stood before Pontius Pilate, He revealed an important principle: "You would have no authority over Me, unless it had been given you from above" (John 19:11). Paul later echoed this concept in Romans 13:1. Write it out below:

_____

_____

_____

_____

_____

_____

_____

_____

_____

_____

_____

_____

This may be difficult to accept, especially if those in leadership are cruel, incompetent, or do not meet your expectations. However, God desires for you to pray for those in authority (1 Timothy 2:1–2). Therefore, intercede on behalf of those who direct you. Likewise, ask the Lord to give you grace and understanding about why He has placed you under their leadership.

A Gift for Today

What you believe about the Lord's power and authority in this world will affect how you view your circumstances.

In the reign of great Caesar, the emp'ror of Rome,
The first work of salvation for sinners was done
By Heaven's decree—for a Babe then was sent
As a ransom for sinners—so let us repent. . . .
Being resolved together to Bethlehem to go;
And when they came thither they found it was so.
So let us be merry in a moderate way,
Sing praises with homage, and honour the day.
The great King of Glory to this world being brought,
God's love for poor sinners with wonder was wrought:
And when they had swaddled our Saviour so sweet,
In an ox's manger they laid him to sleep.
"In the Reign of Great Caesar" published
by William Henry Husk[5]

CHAPTER SEVEN

GOD WITH US

✦

*"She will bear a Son; and you shall call His name Jesus, for He will save His people from their sins." Now all this took place to fulfill what was spoken by the Lord through the prophet: "*Behold, the virgin shall be with child and shall bear a Son, and they shall call His name Immanuel,*" which translated means, "*God with us.*"*

Matthew 1:21–23

I t is easy to miss the significant moments of life—especially when they are cloaked in difficulty and darkness. After all, there was nothing especially meaningful in a couple having a baby—it happens daily. In fact, what seemingly made this particular birth even less momentous was that it lacked the usual fanfare surrounding it—a home carefully prepared for the arrival of the child and family celebrations. Indeed, for those two weary travelers in Bethlehem more than two thousand years ago, the overcrowded town offered no accommodations, so they had to resort to a stable. According to Jewish tradition, Joseph and Mary settled in what would have been a rudimentary cave like those that perforate the hills around Bethlehem today. The young girl would have given birth to her Son on the hard ground of a damp, dark stall, and then would have laid Him in a manger—a stone trough where the animals were usually fed. It appeared very insignificant indeed.

However, the Lord was up to something absolutely awesome because this was the most important, extraordinary, and meaningful birth in the history of humanity—past, present, or future. God Himself took on human flesh to walk among us, to teach us the truth, to show us the way of salvation, and to reveal Himself to us.

More than six hundred years before Jesus' birth, the prophet Isaiah told what His coming would mean to the world: "The Lord Himself will give you a sign: Behold, a virgin will be with child and bear a son, and she will call His name Immanuel" (Isaiah 7:14).

Matthew explained to us that *Immanuel* literally means "God with us" (Matthew 1:23). This baby in the manger was not just another common infant, born to ordinary parents from an irrelevant town. Jesus is God Himself, the Promised One, the Messiah, the Savior of the world, the one and only Son of the living Lord.

We've talked about that throughout this book. But what I want you to see here is that we often mistake how the Father works. We may think of Jesus as being born in peace and comfort. After all, He is the Son of God. We may wonder at the prophesies made about Him or consider how remarkable the heavenly chorus sounded.

However, the harsh reality is that Jesus was born into the lowly setting of a stable, in the discomfort of poverty, in the harsh landscape of Israel, and into a world of political adversity where Rome oppressed and abused the Jews. When Jesus took His first human breath, He did not do so in a palace encircled by silk and perfumes, with servants at the ready. Rather, He was surrounded by the odor of unwashed animals used for the most common tasks. His cradle was an awkward feeding trough filled with straw. His blanket was made of rough and inexpensive swaddling cloth. Why would God choose such a difficult way to be incarnated?

But understand, Jesus came not to impress you but to identify personally with you. He wanted to experience what it was like to be you—and not just on your best days but on your worst. Because of this He was not born the privileged son of a ruler

✳

Jesus wanted to experience what it
was like to be you—and not just on
your best days but on your worst.

with all resources at His disposal. Rather, Isaiah 53:3 tells us, "He was despised and forsaken of men, a man of sorrows and acquainted with grief; and like one from whom men hide their face He was despised, and we did not esteem Him." Jesus knows what it is to be rejected, betrayed, and looked down upon. He knows what it feels like to wrestle with loss, hunger, and pain. He has experienced emotional and physical abuse, alienation, and abandonment firsthand.

Why did Christ choose to endure all of that? Hebrews 2:17–18 explains, "It was necessary for him to be made in every respect like us, his brothers and sisters, so that he could be our merciful and faithful High Priest before God. Then he could offer a sacrifice that would take away the sins of the people. Since he himself has gone through suffering and testing, he is able to help us when we are being tested" (NLT). In other words Jesus chose to be born and exist in the worst conditions so that He could empathize with us and faithfully minister to us, regardless of what we may suffer. He even comprehends the root reasons for why we sin and how to lead us to healing and freedom from its grasp.

With this in mind, it is crucial to meditate on the significance of *God with us*—to consider what His abiding presence means for your life, your identity, and your comprehension of why you are here. When you believe in Jesus as your Savior, you are a child of God, a member of His family, and sealed with His Holy Spirit so that nothing can take you out of His hand. Your life is never without value, purpose, or meaning. You are never alone or helpless. On the contrary, He promises, "Don't be afraid, for I am with you. Don't be discouraged, for I am your God. I will strengthen you and help you. I will hold you up with my victorious right hand" (Isaiah 41:10 NLT).

But also, realize that the true importance of *God with us* is most brilliant in the moments when things don't seem to be going right. We may picture the Lord accompanying us in the victories, successes, and accomplishments of life. When all is well, we recognize His favor—as well we should. But often, when our world falls apart, we tend to assume He is absent. We wonder what we've done to displease Him or even drive Him away. During those times, we may think He has forgotten about us or abandoned us, but nothing could be further from the truth. The Lord is with us most intimately in the midst of our storms—especially when the facade of our self-sufficiency has been washed away. Usually we grow closer to Jesus, learn more about Him, and experience His presence most powerfully in the difficulties of life. Indeed, we know that the character of Christ is born in us through the challenges. As Paul wrote, "We can rejoice . . . when we run into problems and trials, for we know that they help us develop endurance. And endurance develops strength of character, and character strengthens our confident hope of salvation. And this hope will not lead to disappointment. For we know how dearly God loves us, because he has given us the Holy Spirit to fill our hearts with his love" (Romans 5:3–5 NLT).

So regardless of what you may face, remember *God is with*

you! Jesus came that you "may have life, and have it abundantly" (John 10:10). He came to make you a whole person—to give you a new life and a new spirit, to restore whatever sin has shattered, and to renew your mind, will, and emotions. And that is all especially true during your weakest times of testing and trial. So just as Jesus was born into adversity to learn about you—use your times of struggle to know Him better. God is with you! Take comfort in this truth and take note of the significance of those incredibly important moments when the Lord reveals Himself to you through the difficulties.

A Moment of Reflection

What are the areas of life where you find it hardest to believe that God is with you? Write them below.

_____

_____

_____

_____

_____

_____

_____

_____

_____

_____

Pray and ask God how He desires to minister to you in the situations above. As He communicates with you, write what He says below.

_____

_____

_____

_____

In 1 Thessalonians 5:18, Paul instructed, "In everything give thanks; for this is God's will for you in Christ Jesus." Even if the Lord has not revealed His ministry to you in the areas above, give Him thanks. Express your trust that even if you do not see His hand or His purposes in the situations you're experiencing, you know that He is with you and would never abandon you.

_____

_____

_____

_____

A Gift for Today

God does not abandon you in the dark times but draws you closer through them so you can experience His presence and freedom.

"God with us!" O glorious name!
Let it shine in endless fame:
God and man in Christ unite:
O mysterious depth and height!
"God with us," in flesh array'd,
Lower than the angels made;
Made to suffer, to sustain
All our guilt, and curse, and pain.
"God with us!" Amazing love!
Jesus left the realms above;
Took our nature and our place;
Died to save our ruin'd race.
"God with us," though seated high;
Now He reigns above the sky;
Still with us He deigns to dwell,
All our foes and fears to quell,
"God with us!" O wondrous grace!
We shall see Him face to face,
That we may Immanuel sing,
As we ought, our God and King!
"GOD WITH US! O GLORIOUS NAME!" BY SARAH SLINN[6]

CHAPTER EIGHT

GOOD NEWS OF GREAT JOY

. . . . ✦ . . . .

*In the same region there were some shepherds
staying out in the fields and keeping watch
over their flock by night. And an angel
of the Lord suddenly stood before them,
and the glory of the Lord shone around
them; and they were terribly frightened.
But the angel said to them, "Do not be afraid;
for behold, I bring you good news of great
joy which will be for all the people; for today
in the city of David there has been born for
you a Savior, who is Christ the Lord."*

LUKE 2:8–11

One might imagine that for those shepherds in Bethlehem, the night began like any other. With just the moonlight and stars overhead to light their path, the terrain was rocky and difficult to maneuver. Of course it was not much easier to navigate in the daytime, when finding just the right grazing spots and clean water sources for their flocks was essential. Even with their best, most watchful care, sheep could wander from the herd, get into trouble, or become sick, and there was always the danger of thieves and predators. So these shepherds prepared themselves for the unenviable task of keeping watch at night; they hunkered down for the constant, never-ending challenge of tending and protecting their flocks.

With the herds corralled, the beasts rested in peace as these men kept watch. It is conceivable that as the coals of the campfire burned low and the last few embers of the night's fire discharged a glowing warmth, this band of shepherds fought drowsiness and would take turns resting as the sheep quietly rustled about. But as silence settled over the camp, I can imagine those shepherds finally being alone with their thoughts. And I wonder if—when everything got quiet—they wrestled with the epithets attributed to them: *untrustworthy, contemptable, unclean, lowly,* and, ultimately, *unworthy.* We know how those lonely, uninterrupted moments can often surface our worst feelings, fears, and failures.

Sadly, these shepherds knew how poorly they were viewed by others. They realized that some considered them worth less

We know how those lonely,
uninterrupted moments
can often surface our worst
feelings, fears, and failures.

than the sheep they tended. They were branded as sinners, and it seemed that nothing could change how they were perceived. We might imagine the pain they felt, the disrespect they had been shown, and the helplessness of their situation.

But suddenly a brilliant figure appeared before them, illuminating the night sky. An angel of the Lord, radiating the glory of the living God, was suspended above them. He was so imposing and majestic that several members of the group must have fallen on their faces at the sight of him. This was no dream, illusion, or figment of their imaginations. This was real. What judgment would he bring against them? After all, they were mere shepherds—not the great men of God such as Abraham, Moses, and David. They were unclean, sinners. Like Isaiah before the glorious presence of the Lord, perhaps they thought, "Woe is me, for I am ruined! Because I am a man of unclean lips, and I live among a people of unclean lips" (Isaiah 6:5). Certainly, punishment was the only reason for this angel's appearance.

Perhaps they had forgotten that Abraham, Moses, and David had been shepherds as well, so the angel likely proclaimed a very different message from what they expected. The Lord sent His messenger to them because He had an important blessing for them and He did not want them to miss it. So the angel said:

> Do not be afraid; for behold, I bring you good news of great joy which will be for all the people; for today in the city of David there has been born for you a Savior, who is Christ the Lord.

This will be a sign for you: you will find a baby wrapped in cloths and lying in a manger. (Luke 2:10–12)

No sooner had the angel spoken these words than thousands of additional angels joined him and sang the most beautiful, heavenly song the shepherds had ever heard: "Glory to God in the highest, and on earth peace among men with whom He is pleased" (Luke 2:14).

One might imagine the stunned silence that overcame the shepherds the moment that holy concert concluded. They must have looked at one another with wide eyes and questioning faces as their minds worked to understand the awesome message. One thing was for sure—they had just received a great honor, and they knew it. Luke reported,

> When the angels had gone away from them into heaven, the shepherds began saying to one another, "Let us go straight to Bethlehem then, and see this thing that has happened which the Lord has made known to us." So they came in a hurry and found their way to Mary and Joseph, and the baby as He lay in the manger. When they had seen this, they made known the statement which had been told them about this Child. (Luke 2:15–17)

After hearing the angel's message and witnessing the praise and adoration of the heavenly host, the shepherds left their flocks and quickly went to Bethlehem to see what God had made known to them. They believed the message and acted on it.

But what I think is important to always remember is that God did not choose to send His angelic host to a king or a high priest. The Lord did not seek out the most pious group in Bethlehem and give them a solemn charge to spread the Word. Instead, the almighty God sent good news of great joy that would comfort the heart and give hope to the hearers. And He sent this holiest of birth announcements to ordinary shepherds—men who were considered outcasts. In fact, some of the rabbis would lump them in with the likes of tax collectors, robbers, thugs, and those with unethical reputations in financial matters. They were rejected and overlooked because of the humble work they did, which made them ceremonially unclean. And because their labor kept them away from the temple for weeks and months at a time, they had little if any chance to cleanse themselves spiritually.

In other words God went to those who needed Him the most—the poor and humble in spirit. The people who felt forgotten and alone. He came to identify with each of their hurts, and He comes to us in the same way today.

Perhaps there are moments when you feel as overlooked, unworthy, and unclean as those shepherds. Maybe there have been times when people made you feel like you are worthless, unlovable, and unredeemable. It appears as if no one sees how hard you try, how profoundly you hurt, and how much you want

God went to those who needed
Him the most—the poor and
humble in spirit. He came to
identify with each of their
hurts, and He comes to us
in the same way today.

some peace. It could even be that you fear God's presence because you expect judgment, rather than the Father's open arms of love.

Friend, when you feel any of these things, always remember that the Lord God sent His proclamation of salvation to those lowly shepherds *first*. That's because "the LORD is near to the brokenhearted and saves those who are crushed in spirit" (Psalm 34:18). He *always* wants you regardless of whoever else may cast you aside. So follow those shepherds' example and run to the Savior. He always has good news of great joy to share with you.

A Moment of Reflection

Do you ever identify with the shepherds—feeling unworthy, unclean, or unlovable? If so, that is not God's will for you. In Jeremiah 31:3, He says, "I have loved you with an everlasting love; therefore I have drawn you with lovingkindness." With this truth in mind, ask God to help you understand how He truly cares for and values you.

_____

_____

_____

_____

_____

_____

The journey to understanding your worth is never short or easy. It is a lifetime endeavor in which you learn to see yourself as God does. And the main way you do so is by spending time with Him in Scripture. Therefore, read each of the following verses and ask God to give you a true and profound understanding of what they really mean. Write down what He reveals to you.

Psalm 139:1–4:

_____

_____

_____

_____

_____

_____

_____

Psalm 139:13–14:

_____

_____

_____

_____

_____

_____

_____

Psalm 139:16:

_____

_____

_____

_____

_____

_____

_____

_____

Psalm 139:23–24:

_____

_____

_____

_____

_____

_____

_____

A Gift for Today

God loves you just as you are, but He also wants you to understand all the wonderful potential and value He sees in you.

While shepherds watched their flocks by night,
All seated on the ground,
The angel of the LORD came down,
And glory shone around.
"Fear not," said he; for mighty dread
Had seized their troubled mind;
"Glad tidings of great joy I bring
To you and all mankind.
"To you, in David's town this day
Is born of David's line
A SAVIOR who is CHRIST the LORD;
And this shall be the sign;
"The heavenly Babe you there shall find
To human view displayed,
All meanly wrapped in swathing bands
And in a manger laid."
Thus spake the seraph: and forthwith
Appeared a shining throng
Of angels praising GOD, who thus
Addressed their joyful song:
"All glory be to GOD on high,
And in the earth be peace;
Good-will henceforth from heaven to men
Begin and never cease." Amen.

"WHILE SHEPHERDS WATCHED THEIR FLOCKS" BY NAHUM TATE[7]

CHAPTER 9

FROM THE REALMS
OF GLORY

. . . . ✦ . . . . . .

There appeared with the angel a multitude of
the heavenly host praising God and saying,
"Glory to God in the highest, and on earth
peace among men with whom He is pleased."
LUKE 2:13–14

D o you ever wonder what it was like to be among the heavenly host the night the Son of God was born? All heaven knew of the Lord's promises to mankind. At times, these angels even had the privilege of delivering small pieces of the puzzle concerning God's grand mystery of how the Savior would appear. After all, angels were God's servants, His chosen deputies, who were often sent out as His representatives to deliver important tidings to His people. One can imagine their excitement every time another detail was revealed.

On that awesome evening they understood the stakes better than humanity could. They had seen the story from before God even laid the foundation of the earth—how with incredible wisdom and discernment He placed the starry expanse and divided light from darkness, sky from earth, and water from land. They watched as with meticulous detail He created each plant and creature and even breathed Adam's first breath into his lungs. They also saw that awful day when humanity first sinned against the Lord. Did the man and woman not understand how good and wise the Creator was? Did they not realize how they had broken the Father's heart? Did they not grasp that through their actions, the whole human race was poisoned? Every person born thereafter would inherit a sinful nature and would live in disobedience and rebellion toward almighty God that would ultimately lead to death. As Romans 5 explains, "Through one man sin entered into the world, and death through sin, and so death spread to all men, because all sinned" (v. 12).

This heavenly host understood the grave mistake that was made on that day in the garden of Eden. While the Father reaches out in loving-kindness toward us, His holiness requires that our sin be removed from us before we can dwell in His presence. What that means is humanity unwittingly separated itself from the Source of its comfort, provision, security, guidance, and strength. And the angelic host watched as year after year, people invented new ways to reach up to the Lord—and failed miserably in doing so. Sin was the barrier human effort and ingenuity could not possibly overcome.

Certainly there is nothing we as people can ever do to remove our own sin, although we may try. Often we have trouble even stopping ourselves from certain transgressions—doubt, fear, pride, self-centeredness, and all the others that are so deeply ingrained in humanity. Because of this, the godly apostle Paul lamented, "I want to do what is good, but I don't. I don't want to do what is wrong, but I do it anyway. But if I do what I don't want to do, I am not really the one doing wrong; it is sin living in me that does it" (Romans 7:19–20 NLT). Indeed, even when we attempt to keep all the rules of holiness, we may unwittingly violate the commands we do not know or that are perplexing to us. There are also the complex situations that can make good people disagree—who can discern and avoid what is iniquity then? We make our best guesses and then forever wonder if we took the right path.

Watching all of our struggles throughout history, the angelic

Sin was the barrier human effort and ingenuity could not possibly overcome.

host recognized that we were helpless to rectify our fallen situation—even when we didn't understand. And that meant they realized we were eternally doomed to separation from God, suffering an everlasting punishment that we could scarce imagine even on our worst days.

But they also saw that God, who is infinitely just and loving in every circumstance, would find a way. How would the Lord, who is self-governed by His own principles of righteousness, extend love and forgiveness to humanity? This was not a task for kings, priests, prophets, or even His most dedicated and capable angels. This mission was so important that God Himself would come to earth to make sure it was accomplished. Jesus, the sinless, perfect God, came into the world to die on the cross, to be the sacrifice for our sin.

Surely this was an inconceivably important and awesome endeavor of the living God—an eternity-shaking mission that deserved to be heralded with the finest heavenly praise. So when the angel of the Lord was done proclaiming the good news of great joy to the shepherds of Bethlehem, the multitude of the heavenly host burst forth in praise to the Lord, who is so good and loving: "Glory to God in the highest, and on earth peace among men with whom He is pleased" (Luke 2:14). Finally, humanity would be reconciled—have peace and fellowship—with the Lord God when Jesus removed our sin. No doubt the angels hoped the world would understand and appreciate the splendor and majesty of that holy moment. It truly was amazingly good news of great

This was an eternity-shaking
mission that deserved
to be heralded with the
finest heavenly praise.

and eternal joy for whoever would recognize the incredible love of the living God.

Today, take note of the attitude of the ones who have known the Lord for longer than we can imagine, who have consistently served in His presence throughout the ages, and who have seen His activity from a perspective far above our own. This angelic host worships before Him day and night because of how exceptionally awesome He is. That heavenly concert to the shepherds was merely a glimpse of the vast and glorious service of worship that continues for all time because the Lord indisputably deserves nothing less—that is how worthy, loving, and wise He is. And the angels have been God's faithful ambassadors all along the way—seeing the magnificent insight with which He interacts with His creation and longing to be part of His plan. They know the secret that would be prudent for us to learn: "God causes all things to work together for good to those who love God, to those who are called according to His purpose" (Romans 8:28). His plan is brilliant, and we can trust His loving heart even when our circumstances are difficult.

Therefore, I pray that this Christmas—regardless of what you are facing—you will join the heavenly host and proclaim, "Glory to God in the highest!" Certainly He is worthy of your praise and is working all things out in a way that will bring you His peace and great joy.

A Moment of Reflection

Think about a time in your life when you went through a challenge, but God used it for good. Write about it below.

_____

_____

_____

_____

How did God change your situation? Praise Him for all the ways He redeemed it and for the blessings that came from it.

_____

_____

_____

_____

_____

Are there any circumstances in your life right now that appear too difficult to turn for good? Give that situation to God and spend time praising Him for all the ways He has helped you in the past.

_____

_____

_____

_____

_____

A Gift for Today

If you will maintain focus on God during times of adversity and continue to praise Him, not only will you grow closer to Him, but you will find some blessing in everything you go through.

Angels, from the realms of glory,
Wing your flight o'er all the earth;
Ye who sang creation's story,
Now proclaim Messiah's birth:
Come and worship, come and worship,
Worship Christ, the newborn King . . .
Though an infant now we view him,
He shall fill his Father's throne,
Gather all the nations to him;
Ev'ry knee shall then bow down:
Come and worship, come and worship,
Worship Christ, the newborn King.
All creation, join in praising
God, the Father, Spirit, Son,
Evermore your voices raising,
To the eternal Three-in-One:
Come and worship, come and worship,
Worship Christ, the newborn King.

"ANGELS, FROM THE REALMS OF GLORY" BY JAMES MONTGOMERY[8]

CHAPTER TEN

THE LAMB OF GOD

You were not redeemed with perishable things like silver or gold from your futile way of life inherited from your forefathers, but with precious blood, as of a lamb unblemished and spotless, the blood of Christ.

1 PETER 1:18–19

When Mary held Jesus in her arms for the first time and looked into His sweet face, I wonder what she thought. I am certain she was full of love and hopefulness for her baby. She may have recalled Gabriel's amazing words, "He will be great and will be called the Son of the Most High; and the Lord God will give Him the throne of His father David; and He will reign over the house of Jacob forever, and His kingdom will have no end" (Luke 1:32–33). Despite the less-than-optimal surroundings, when she thought about God's promise, the days ahead most likely looked bright.

Whereas the futures of most newborns appear full of unknowns, this sweet child's purpose was set from before the foundation of the world. Before any other creature was formed, God's plan for Christ was established and unmovable. His incarnation would be the pivot point of all history and would lay the foundation for Him to become the object of worship for all mankind. This baby who slept in His mother's arms so defenseless and weak, who seemingly had so little value that He was laid in a dirty feeding trough, was (and is) the most powerful Force in human history. He would split time right down the middle.

What perhaps Mary did not realize was that Jesus would do so by sacrificing Himself so that we could have eternal life. Christ came not only to preach, to teach, and to heal—although those were important aspects of His ministry. Rather, before the Lord laid the first handful of rock and soil on this globe and before anything was ever created, He determined that Jesus Christ, His only begotten Son, would come into this world and die for your sins and mine. He came "to give His life a ransom for many," a sacrificial substitute for our lives (Matthew 20:28).

This was because God foresaw that humanity would sin against Him before He ever created Adam and Eve—and He prepared in advance for our redemption. From the beginning, because of His great love for us, the Lord assumed responsibility for covering our sins. In the garden of Eden, following Adam and Eve's disobedience, God sacrificed an animal and used the skin to clothe them (Genesis 3:21). God furnished a ram for Abraham to present as a substitute offering for Isaac, Abraham's son (22:13). The Lord used the blood of physically spotless lambs to protect the children of Israel when the death angel swept through Egypt and claimed the firstborn son of every household (Exodus 12:1–13).

The lamb became the symbol of sacrifice throughout the Old Testament, with more than eighty references in Exodus, Leviticus, and Numbers alone addressing their use. Perhaps this is why Jesus was born among the other rams and ewes in the stable—because He would be the ultimate Lamb of God.

You see, the Lord had made it clear: "Without shedding of blood there is no forgiveness" (Hebrews 9:22). Although the blood of animals covered sin, it could not completely erase it. And because all people "have sinned and fall short of the glory of God," shedding our own blood could never take away the great cost of our fallenness either, because our blood is stained by our transgressions (Romans 3:23; 5:12). But Jesus was conceived by

Jesus was born among the other rams and ewes in the stable—because He would be the ultimate Lamb of God.

the Holy Spirit and was virgin-born, which means He could be the absolutely blameless Lamb of God, without spot or blemish either physically or spiritually. In other words He was perfectly holy—completely sinless—and He would continue to be so throughout His life.

Therefore, it was quite natural for Isaiah to picture the Messiah "like a lamb that is led to slaughter, and like a sheep that is silent before its shearers, so He did not open His mouth" (Isaiah 53:7). This Lamb became the sacrificial offering for our sin, paying the penalty we could never afford and providing for our pardon. This is why John, the forerunner of Christ, proclaimed, "Behold, the Lamb of God who takes away the sin of the world!" (John 1:29).

Christ did not come as a commanding general with a tremendous army, as a great military strategist, nor as a king or great leader of humanity—at least, not on this first visit. Rather, He appeared in the likeness of a creature characterized by innocence and gentleness, known for its role in the sacrifice. Jesus came to lay His life down that our sins might be forgiven and we could be clothed in His righteousness for all eternity—a promise He fulfilled when He died on the cross and rose again from the grave.

The real importance of that scene in Bethlehem was not the three wise men, the shepherd boys, the host of angels, or the animals that surrounded the manger. Rather, Bethlehem was the birthplace of the Lamb, the hope of all mankind.

But there is something important for you to see here. It is one thing to say Jesus Christ came into the world to save all people from their sins, but it is entirely different to be able to grasp it as *personal*—to understand in a profound way within your spirit that God the Father sent His only Son into the world to save *you*.

When Mary looked into Jesus' face, she looked at Him with love. It was personal. He was not only real to her, but her heart belonged to Him. When you look at Jesus—whether it is while you read Scripture, pray, or simply meditate about who He is—what do you feel about Him? Is He distant, mysterious, or seemingly unknowable? Or is He personal to you—your whole being filled with love and gratefulness toward the One who took your sins away? Is He simply a person you read about—like any other figure throughout history? Or is He your treasure, who possesses your whole heart, soul, mind, and strength?

I pray that as you meditate on Christ and consider who He is, you will accept Him as your Lamb who takes away all your sin. That as you look into His face, like Mary, you will see the hopefulness and joy His life brings. For He truly is gentle and humble in heart, and in Him, you will find rest for your soul (Matthew 11:29).

A Moment of Reflection

At times, people envision the Lord as an overbearing taskmaster because of the sacrifices He demanded in the Old Testament.

Yet He required those offerings to show how we could not save ourselves. When Jesus came as the Lamb of God, we saw a very different side to the Lord—we understood that Christ was the ultimate offering God required to take away *all* our sin forever. Have you ever accepted Jesus' loving sacrifice for you? If yes, write your testimony below. If no, but you want to, write out a simple prayer asking Jesus to be your Savior.

_____

_____

_____

_____

_____

_____

Jesus is the only way to know the Father. And the awesome thing about the salvation He offers is that all He requires of us is to believe in Him. Romans 10:9 tells us how to show that we trust in Jesus for salvation: "If you confess with your mouth Jesus as Lord, and believe in your heart that God raised Him from the dead, you will be saved." Therefore, as soon as possible, call someone who you know is a Christian and tell them that Jesus is your Lord and that you believe that even though Jesus died on the cross, He rose from the grave in order to forgive you of your sins. Write down who you called and the date below.

_____

_____

———————————————————————————————

———————————————————————————————

———————————————————————————————

———————————————————————————————

———————————————————————————————

———————————————————————————————

———————————————————————————————

A Gift for Today

Knowing Jesus as your Savior means you never have to feel unworthy or shameful when approaching the Lord—you are absolutely forgiven, completely accepted, and utterly cleansed of all you've ever done wrong.

Come, behold the Virgin Mother,
Fondly leaning on her child,
Nature shows not such another.
Glorious, holy, meek and mild.
Bethlehem's ancient walls enclose Him,
Dwelling place of David once;
Now no friendly homestead knows Him,
Tho' the noblest of his sons. . . .
Why, ah, why this condescension,

God with mortal man to dwell?
Why lay by His grand pretension,
He who does all thrones excel?
'Tis to be a man, a brother,
With us sinners of mankind:
Vain we search for such another,
Ne'er we love like this shall find.
'Tis to make Himself an offering
As a pure atoning lamb,
Souls redeeming by His suffering,
That in human flesh He came;
As a God He could not suffer,
He a body true must have;
As a man what He might offer
Could not satisfy or save. . . .
May we now, that day forestalling,
Hear the word, and read and pray,
Listen to the Gospel calling,
And with humble heart obey.
Give us hearty true repentance,
Live in faith and holiness;
Then we need not fear Thy sentence,
But may trust Thy saving grace,
Hallelujah, Hallelujah, Hallelujah,
Praise the Lord.

"THE BABE OF BETHLEHEM" PUBLISHED BY WILLIAM HENRY HUSK[9]

CHAPTER ELEVEN

A TURNING POINT

* * * * * * ✳ * * * * * *

*There was the true Light which, coming into
the world, enlightens every man. He was in
the world, and the world was made through
Him, and the world did not know Him . . .
But as many as received Him, to them He
gave the right to become children of God,
even to those who believe in His name.*

JOHN 1:9–10, 12

At times, people celebrate the birth of Christ, they think about baby Jesus in the manger, December 25th comes and goes, and that is it. The focus of their celebrations turns to the New Year. Of course, we know that Christ came with a great mission to die on the cross for our sins and reconcile us to God. But in terms of our calendar, we may mark off the day and move on.

But even better than the New Year, Christmas marks our spiritual and eternal beginning, our new life, and especially our new relationship with God. As 2 Corinthians 5:17 teaches us, "If anyone is in Christ, he is a new creature; the old things passed away; behold, new things have come." Because of this, what we need to comprehend is that Jesus did not come to be celebrated on *one* day a year—He came to shed light on and transform *every* day of our lives. If Christmas does not remind us of all that is possible now that Christ has repaired our relationship with God and shown us who He truly is, then we have missed the point completely.

The truth is knowing Jesus can change absolutely everything for you. No, your immediate circumstances may not be what you want them to be. But He can give you the strength and wisdom to navigate them, give you spiritual insight, and change your life for the better through them. He will also mold your character and heal your belief system—purging the bad and building the godly and eternal in you. And, of course, your relationship with Him will determine your eternal destination, which can and should transform how you experience situations.

✳

Knowing Jesus can change
absolutely everything for you.

You see, when it was time to launch His ministry, Jesus, filled with the Holy Spirit, began preaching that "the kingdom of heaven is at hand" (Matthew 4:17). He wanted the people to know there is another dominion—a far better realm and way to live—that He was establishing. This is not like the other empires of the world that would divide and conquer; rule and oppress; emerge and decline. Rather, Jesus' domain is everlasting, frees its citizens, and overcomes all cultural, racial, generational, socioeconomic, and internal and external divisions. And Christ not only enlightened us to the principles of His everlasting kingdom but also empowered us to live them.

Jesus shed light on the ways of heaven, showing us how to live and think in a completely different way, with a fresh perspective and goal. Of course, this does not happen easily, and He said some difficult things that may be challenging for us to accept. For example, He instructed, "Whoever hits you on the cheek, offer him the other also; and whoever takes away your coat, do not withhold your shirt from him either" (Luke 6:29). Indeed, what Jesus said often appeared counterintuitive and paradoxical. In another instance He taught we should always forgive, that it is more blessed to give than receive, and that "whoever wishes to save his life will lose it; but whoever loses his life for My sake will find it" (Matthew 16:25).

The people had never heard such things, and they had never experienced teaching with this kind of authority—it was obvious Jesus was no ordinary rabbi. Indeed, those who heard Him might have been skeptical, but they could not deny the miracles Christ performed. At Jesus' command, the blind could see, the deaf could hear, and the paralyzed could walk. He healed all kinds of sickness and cast out demons. Thousands were fed with just a few loaves of bread and a handful of fish. He walked on water, calmed the raging sea, and even raised the dead. There was no refuting His supernatural supremacy. The crowd flocked to Him, eager for His touch. In fact, we learn that healing was imparted merely by touching the hem of His garment. What Jesus promised came. to be, what He said was true, and what He commanded was right and powerful.

Those who saw Christ and walked in His light understood the awesome blessing of His presence—and you can too. Of course, it may seem like a long time ago when all this happened, but Jesus is just as near to you today through the presence of Holy Spirit. This is why Paul wrote:

> We have not ceased to pray for you and to ask that you may be filled with the knowledge of His will in all spiritual wisdom and understanding, so that you will walk in a manner worthy of the Lord, to please Him in all respects, bearing fruit in every good work and increasing in the knowledge of God; strengthened with all power, according to His glorious might, for the attaining of all steadfastness and patience; joyously giving thanks to the Father, who has qualified us to share in the inheritance of the saints in Light. For He rescued us from

the domain of darkness, and transferred us to the kingdom of His beloved Son. (Colossians 1:9–13)

In other words, there are so many blessings you receive as a citizen of God's sovereign reign, and the Lord doesn't want you to miss any of them. He doesn't rescue you from the domain of darkness, transfer you to His kingdom, and give you His light just to then abandon you. Rather, He "gives us the victory through our Lord Jesus Christ" (1 Corinthians 15:57). Jesus wants to give you a new mind and supernatural insight into His will and His ways. He wants to walk with you, illuminate your path, enlighten you to the potential He built in you, and lead you in a life that is far more significant and fulfilling than anything you could possibly imagine. You exist for a cause that is so much greater and more important than yourself or this world. You are called to live for Jesus Christ and for His kingdom, bearing witness to who He is in your life. And when you do, He promises that your joy will be full (John 15:11) and you will bear "lasting fruit" (v. 16 NLT).

But you have to make the choice to live for Him in the way He leads you to live. Jesus said, "The kingdom of heaven is like a treasure hidden in the field, which a man found and hid again; and from joy over it he goes and sells all that he has and buys that field" (Matthew 13:44). In other words, the value of what Jesus offers you should inspire you to make a radical choice about what is truly important in your life. Paul said it this way: "Whatever things were gain to me, those things I have counted as loss for the sake of Christ. More than that, I count all things to be loss in view of the surpassing value of knowing Christ Jesus my Lord" (Philippians 3:7–8). Paul comprehended that what he thought gave him value and worth—such as all the ways he tried to build his own kingdom—were rubbish compared to the absolute treasure of knowing Jesus and participating in His kingdom.

Therefore, understanding the truth of who Christ is means you are confronted with a decision: Will you continue on your own path, seeking what only your limited human mind and abilities can achieve? Or will you believe the testimony of Scripture about who Jesus is, accept Him as Lord of your life, and follow Him wholeheartedly? Will you check December 25 off your calendar and turn your thoughts to the New Year? Or will the birth of Christ remind you that "the kingdom of God is in your midst" (Luke 17:21), that He instituted a new way to live, and that He deserves your complete allegiance?

Friend, you know the answer. Even now, the Holy Spirit is speaking to your heart about the hopefulness of giving Christ 100 percent of your life. Do not be afraid to turn from the darkness and brokenness of this world to follow the One who will never lead you astray. Instead, as Proverbs 3:5–6 instructs, "Trust in the LORD with all your heart and do not lean on your own understanding. In all your ways acknowledge Him, and He will make your paths straight." Let Jesus light your path and show you all that is possible.

A Moment of Reflection

Is there anything Jesus taught that is difficult for you to obey? Write it below.

_____

_____

_____

_____

_____

_____

_____

_____

What is keeping you from obeying Christ wholeheartedly? Ask God to show you the root of what is standing in the way of following Him completely and seeing the kingdom of heaven lived out through you.

_____

_____

_____

_____

_____

_____

_____

_____

_____

A Gift for Today

Jesus makes you brand new, and if you will heed what He says, He will lead you to the abundant life for which you long.

> *Born Thy people to deliver,*
> *Born a child and yet a King,*
> *Born to reign in us forever,*
> *Now Thy gracious kingdom bring.*
> *By Thine own eternal Spirit*
> *Rule in all our hearts alone;*
> *By Thine all sufficient merit,*
> *Raise us to Thy glorious throne.*
>
> "Come, Thou Long-Expected Jesus" by Charles Wesley[10]

CHAPTER TWELVE

BEYOND SAVIOR

✦

· · · · · · ✦ · · · · · ·

His name will be called Wonderful Counselor,
Mighty God, Eternal Father, Prince of Peace.
ISAIAH 9:6

Why is it that some people experience the Christian life as an exciting journey and other people see it as a tiresome, unfulfilling, uncertain, and burdensome path that they must endure? Why is it that some believers appear to have peace and joy in a consistent manner regardless of what they face, and others cannot seem to grasp it very long at all? Why is it that some are able to face the difficulties of life, come out better from them, and have confidence and assurance, while others find themselves consistently plagued with doubt and failure?

Of course, the reasons differ for each person. Some of it has to do with what we just discussed—living for God's kingdom rather than anything this world can offer. But I think one of the main underlying causes is that many people have a very inadequate, impoverished view of who Jesus is. They do not grasp all He is and all He desires to be to us. In fact, there are more than two hundred names for Christ in Scripture, including the Lion of Judah, the Rose of Sharon, the Bright Morning Star, the Good Shepherd, the Great Physician, and the King of kings and Lord of lords.

Unfortunately, many people's knowledge of Jesus stops at His forgiveness for their sins. They don't comprehend what He's up to in their lives or in the world. They understand Christ's role as their Savior and may even strive to obey His commands, but somehow, they never go beyond that—connecting to who He is in an intimate way in their daily lives. We see this in the struggles many believers experience. So many feel alone, without purpose, hopeless, empty, fearful, and rejected. Perhaps you've experienced those emotions and recognize what so many are going through. Maybe like them, you would say, "I wish I had somebody I could go to who understands me; someone I could open my heart to and know that I am accepted; someone who could truly help me overcome and be better." It could also be that you are in the process of making a tremendous decision, feel trapped in your circumstances, or simply wish that someone would walk with you through the challenges you face.

If so, I have a word of encouragement for you. Jesus is all that and can be so much more to you. The prophet Isaiah told us, "A child will be born to us, a son will be given to us; and the government will rest on His shoulders; and His name will be called Wonderful Counselor, Mighty God, Eternal Father, Prince of Peace" (Isaiah 9:6). We know, of course, that the child born and the Son given is Jesus. By placing the government on His shoulders, Isaiah affirmed that Christ has the full authority of the kingdom of heaven, which we spoke about in the last chapter. But the part of interest to us here is that "His name will be called Wonderful Counselor, Mighty God, Eternal Father, Prince of Peace." Let's take a look at what Isaiah meant.

Wonderful Counselor. The reason we need counselors today is because of the sin, hurt, sickness, and sorrow that have resulted from the deceptive guidance the Serpent gave to Eve in the garden of Eden. The Enemy instructed Eve to act independently of God, and what resulted has been the root of all the relational

*

I have Someone who
understands me; Someone
I can open my heart to and
know that I am accepted.

and spiritual pain in this world. We operate without Him, though His wisdom and comprehension are unfathomable and could benefit us without measure.

This is why Isaiah told us that Jesus will be our Wonderful Counselor. The word Isaiah used for *wonderful* is better translated as a wonder, above the ordinary, supernatural, or extraordinary. This is because Jesus is unlike us. He is other—separate from us. Although He knows us intimately, His solutions are nothing we could even conceive of. We learn in Isaiah 55:8–9, "'My thoughts are not your thoughts, nor are your ways My ways,' declares the LORD. 'For as the heavens are higher than the earth, so are My ways higher than your ways and My thoughts than your thoughts.'"

Indeed, Jesus is *omniscient*—He is all-knowing. So when He advises you and instructs you in the best path to take, He does so with absolutely perfect knowledge and wisdom. Think about the astounding privilege you have—the One who created the universe and moves the nations is your Counselor. And He does not instruct you in an overbearing, deceptive, or coercive way, but with truth and wisdom—understanding what you can handle and how best to communicate it to you.

Mighty God. Of course, we have already spoken of the fact that Jesus is God. But Isaiah called Him *El Gibbor*—the conquering, divine Champion and the valiant, victorious Warrior. The One who counsels you is also the One who never fails or loses because He is *omnipotent*—all-powerful. Therefore, Paul declared, "Thanks be to God, who always leads us in triumph in

Christ" (2 Corinthians 2:14). Not only does He have the wisdom to direct you in the best way, He also has the ability to ensure that nothing will thwart His plans for you. He has the capacity to do whatever is required to help you.

Eternal Father. This may sound like a strange title for Jesus. But Christ is the One who gives birth to eternity in you. After all, "When you were dead in your transgressions . . . He made you alive together with Him" (Colossians 2:13). Of course, no theologian or philosopher has ever been able to fathom what it means to be everlasting because it is beyond human comprehension. We function in terms of time—past, present, future; beginnings and endings; and defined seasons. But the Lord functions outside of time. Therefore, there may be events of which you are unaware that your parents, grandparents, and great-grandparents endured that continue to affect you today. You may have no knowledge of them, but the Lord understands fully what they are and how to heal you of them. Likewise, there are decisions you make each day that will impact future generations in ways you cannot conceive. You may be blind to them, but God has each in view and can direct you in them because He is *omnipresent*—He is in every moment and in every place always. Because of this, He will never fail nor forsake you. He knows the end of every situation you experience before it even begins, is present for every decision and action that affects you, and protects you from harm you never saw coming and perhaps never even knew existed.

And that is why He is rightly called *Prince of Peace.* Jesus is

Think about the astounding
privilege you have—the One
who created the universe
and moves the nations
is your Counselor.

omnibenevolent—unconditional and perfect in His love for you. He always has a good, kind, holy, and affectionate heart toward you, so you can count on Jesus to do the right thing 100 percent of the time. And understanding that He is always with you, that He has the wisdom and power to help you, and that He cares about you so much should fill you with peace. As Romans 8:31–32 reminds us, "If God is for us, who is against us? He who did not spare His own Son, but delivered Him over for us all, how will He not also with Him freely give us all things?"

Friend, each of us has tried to meet our own needs in our own ways. We know the anxiety that comes from feeling boxed in without hope. We also know the release we experience when we go to Jesus by faith in prayer and know that He hears every word—even the ones that stay hidden in our hearts. That is what He wants from each of us. He wants us to experience Him in every area of life and trust Him with all the challenges we face. Do not wait until you are out of options. Go to Him first.

Jesus knows there will be times that you will struggle with overwhelming feelings of doubt, fear, hopelessness, and disillusionment. He is aware of every pain, every area of loneliness, hurt, and frustration. However, His message to you is not of anxiety or defeat; rather, it is filled with hope: "These things I have spoken to you, so that in Me you may have peace. In the world you have tribulation, but take courage; I have overcome the world" (John 16:33). Therefore, whatever turmoil, conflict, or personal war you are facing, trust that His words are as true today as they were when He first shared them. Get to know Jesus for who He really is and take comfort in His overwhelming love toward you. And experience the abundant joy, hope, and wonder in the Christian life for which you were created.

A Moment of Reflection

Consider the names of Christ.

Advocate	*Mediator*
Alpha and Omega	*Messiah*
Author and Perfector of our faith	*Mighty God*
Bread of Life	*Prince of Peace*
Bridegroom	*Redeemer*
Bright Morning Star	*Righteous Judge*
Deliverer	*Rose of Sharon*
Everlasting Father	*Savior*
Faithful and True	*Son of God*
Good Shepherd	*Son of Man*
Great Physician	*Suffering Servant*
Immanuel	*Teacher*
King of kings and Lord of lords	*The Way, the Truth, and the Life*
Lamb of God	*Wonderful Counselor*
Lion of Judah	*Word of God*

Those are just a few of the names Christ is called in Scripture. What names of Jesus are most meaningful to you? List them below and describe why they are so significant.

_____

_____

_____

_____

_____

_____

_____

_____

_____

_____

Spend time asking Jesus to know Him by the names that are not so familiar to you and praise Him for who He is.

_____

_____

_____

_____

_____

_____

_____

_____

_____

_____

A Gift for Today

The wonderful thing about Jesus is that the more you get to know Him, the more amazed you'll be at how truly awesome and praiseworthy He is, and the more profoundly He will satisfy your soul.

To us a Child of hope is born,
To us a Son is giv'n,
Him shall the tribes of earth obey,
Him all the hosts of heav'n.
His Name shall be the Prince of Peace,
Forevermore adorned,
The Wonderful, the Counselor,
The great and mighty Lord.
His pow'r, increasing, still shall spread,
His reign no end shall know,
Justice shall guard His throne above,
And peace abound below.
"To Us a Child of Hope Is Born" by John Morrison[11]

CHAPTER THIRTEEN

THE GIFT-MAKER

* * * * * * ✦ * * * * * *

He said to him, "Follow Me." And
he left everything behind, and got
up and began to follow Him.

LUKE 5:27–28

W e often talk about God as the Gift-giver and Jesus as the
greatest Gift ever given—and it is right for us to do so.
But a frequently overlooked ministry is that which belongs to
the Holy Spirit, who is the awesome Gift-*maker*. He has a very
special role in our lives because He conforms us to the character
of Christ and molds us into a blessing for others.

In fact, 1 Corinthians 12:7 teaches, "To each one is given the
manifestation of the Spirit for the common good." Or as the New
Living Translation puts it, "A spiritual gift is given to each of us
so we can help each other." In other words God has given you
tools that He will work through to impact others. He desires for
you to reflect His nature—that you might represent Him on this
earth, doing the work that He desires to accomplish. And when
you allow His Holy Spirit to work through your personality and
giftedness, you become a vessel of His love in action—His hands
and feet in a world that desperately needs to know Him.

Naturally there will be some reading this who are skeptical.
You may think, *I probably couldn't do much good—I can't even
really get my own life straight.* Or, *You don't know my past—I
doubt the Lord wants me representing Him.* But nothing could be
further from the truth. Consider the immense things the Lord
did through Abraham and Jacob, even though both were guilty
of dishonesty (Genesis 20; 27). Remember how powerfully God
used Moses and David though both had committed murder
(Exodus 2:11–14; 2 Samuel 12:9). And think about how much
He worked through the apostle Paul even though he mercilessly

persecuted Christians before he met Jesus. The Lord redeems lives. He delights to work through whomever will trust in Him—regardless of their past.

Consider Levi, a man who made his living as a tax collector. Of course, none of us like it much when the government takes part of our paychecks. But in Jesus' day, tax collectors were among the most despised individuals in Jewish society. They were viewed as traitors and treated as social outcasts because they were Jews recruited by the Roman government to collect duties from other Jews. In other words, they served the enemy in order to get rich themselves.

You see, any monies they gathered above what Rome required, they could keep. So they became wealthy by extorting their fellow countrymen. Further, their constant contact with Gentiles and failure to worship and sacrifice in the temple made them even more undesirable to other Jews. To many, Levi was just a greedy sellout and thief. Levi likely experienced what it felt like to be judged, rejected, shamed, inadequate, and unworthy. He probably never imagined God would single him out for service. It is doubtful those who knew him would have either.

Yet Scripture tells us, "As [Jesus] passed by, He saw Levi the son of Alphaeus sitting in the tax booth, and He said to him, 'Follow Me!' And he got up and followed Him" (Mark 2:14). Jesus knew the truth about Levi, just as He does about each one of us. He recognized Levi's private struggles—his heartaches, faults, failings, and insecurities. He was aware of the times Levi

The Lord delights to
work through whomever
will trust in Him—
regardless of their past.

wrestled with feelings of worthlessness, fear, and loneliness. He also understood the tears Levi cried when no one else was near, and He discerned the hidden longing of Levi's heart—to be loved and accepted by God. Jesus also realized that His decision to add Levi to His band of disciples would be criticized. But Jesus still chose him.

Why? Because Jesus knows how His indwelling Holy Spirit can absolutely transform a soul. So in calling Levi, the Lord did something that He had done before—He changed Levi's name. No one knows when this occurred, but we can imagine it came quickly as a result of his obedient response to Jesus' invitation. After all, the decision to leave the things that were familiar and comfortable must have been difficult for Levi, but it was necessary. It likely isolated him even more from family, and now he would also have to face the rejection of the few friends he had gained among the Roman publicans. The income he made collecting taxes was substantial and probably provided a comfortable existence. But as he no doubt learned, money cannot buy dignity, worth, or joy. And it certainly cannot purchase the peace that comes from being in a right relationship with God. So Scripture makes it clear that Levi got up and left his former occupation without so much as a backward glance. Luke 5:28 states, "He left everything behind, and got up and began to follow Him."

Levi left everything immediately. Jesus was worth it. Christ was unlike anyone Levi had ever met. The Son of God had touched his life with truth, hope, and promise, and it was enough for Levi to make a complete change of course.

So Jesus chose a new name for His disciple—*Matthew,* which means "the gift of God." As Levi, he was a person characterized by taking, but as Matthew, he would give his life away so others could know Christ and take hold of eternal life. He truly became a blessing to others. He traveled with Jesus, recorded the events of Christ's life, and later assembled the information he had gathered into what we know today as the Gospel of Matthew. His account bridges the Old and New Testaments with overwhelming evidence that Jesus Christ is the Jewish Messiah fulfilling the prophesies of old. Matthew also spread the good news of salvation through Jesus to Parthia and Ethiopia, where he was eventually martyred for his faith.

Christ made Matthew into a gift for others, and He can do so for you too. As a believer, you are specially chosen, called, endowed, and empowered by God to love and serve Him. And, like Matthew, the Holy Spirit can work through you to be a witness of His love and forgiveness to a lost and a dying world. The Holy Spirit does so through the spiritual gifts He gives you, such as proclaiming the truth, giving, shepherding, showing mercy, serving, organization, teaching, and exhortation. But He also makes you a blessing by the fruit He produces through you: "love, joy, peace, patience, kindness, goodness, faithfulness, gentleness, [and] self-control" (Galatians 5:22–23). You begin to reflect Jesus' compassion, love, and mercy to others, and they catch a glimpse of the Savior their souls long for. You lead others to Jesus and, in doing so, bring Him credit, honor, and glory.

Proverbs 11:25 promises, "The generous will prosper; those who refresh others will themselves be refreshed" (NLT). There is reward and fulfillment in serving God that simply cannot be experienced any other way because the Lord is working through you to impact eternity. Indeed, the most important thing you can do outside of accepting Christ as your Savior is to give your life to Him and allow Him to lead you each day. So make the choice and open yourself to the possibility of being God's gift to those around you. You will be astounded at the great things He does in and through your life.

A Moment of Reflection

Have you ever had your spiritual gifts assessed? Do you know what your special talents and abilities are? Write them below as well as the strengths God has given you.

_____

_____

_____

_____

_____

_____

_____

Have you ever asked God to make you a gift and blessing to others? Spend time today asking Him to open your eyes to the opportunities for service He has for you.

_____

_____

_____

_____

_____

_____

_____

_____

_____

_____

Look back at your initial list of gifts, talents, and strengths. Are there any the Lord highlighted during your prayer time? If so, offer them to Him for His use.

_____

_____

_____

_____

_____

_____

_____

_____

_____

_____

A Gift for Today

No matter how you view yourself, when God looks at you, He sees all the potential He packed into you and all the good He wants to do through you.

Joyful, joyful, we adore Thee
God of glory, Lord of love
Hearts unfold like flow'rs before Thee
Op'ning to the Sun above
Melt the clouds of sin and sadness
drive the dark of doubt away
Giver of immortal gladness
fill us with the light of day . . .
Mortals join the mighty chorus
which the morning stars began
Father-love is reigning o'er us
brother-love binds man to man.
Ever singing, march we onward
victors in the midst of strife
joyful music lifts us sunward
in the triumph song of life.
"THE HYMN OF JOY" BY HENRY VAN DYKE[12]

CHAPTER 14

WORSHIP THE RETURNING KING

· · · · · · · ✦ · · · · · · ·

"Where is He who has been born King of the Jews? For we saw His star in the east and have come to worship Him."

MATTHEW 2:2

Throughout these pages I have encouraged you to reflect on who Jesus is. I hope it has been a joy to think about what Christmas really means and the great journey the Lord took out of love for you. But as we have seen, Jesus' life did not begin at His birth. And as we know, it did not end at His death either. The resurrection shows us that our Savior is alive and active in our world—His ministry to us continues even though He has ascended to heaven. He sits at the right hand of the Father as He works on our behalf, implementing His plans and ensuring His purposes are fulfilled on this earth.

This continuation is anticipated in Scripture. As we've discussed, Jesus Christ's birth was prophesied by many godly and faithful men throughout the Old Testament. However, that was not the only appearance they talked about. The prophets also foretold a time when Jesus would return to earth—coming again to take His rightful place as the King of kings and Lord of lords. So just as Christmas is a powerful reminder that God has kept His promise to come to our aid, it should also prompt us to remember that He will fulfill every prophecy about returning, defending His people, and establishing His reign.

Indeed, the most exciting part for us is still to come. And the truth is that many of us have lived long enough to see the stage being set for the return of the Lord Jesus Christ. For example, the reestablishment of Israel as a nation is a fulfilled prophecy that needed to occur before His reappearance. Of course, we still do not know when Jesus is coming back. But one thing is certain: it could happen at any moment, and we need to be ready for it—diligently watching for Him and faithfully obeying God until He comes.

So the question each of us must answer is, *Am I ready?* Naturally, the very next question is, *If I am not, how do I get ready?*

Unquestionably, the first step is to make sure you are right with God—that you know Jesus as your Savior and that you've confessed any known sin. But the second is to ensure He has the right place in your life. After all, Christ is coming back as the ultimate Sovereign of all creation. Philippians 2:10 affirms that "at the name of Jesus EVERY KNEE WILL BOW, of those who are in heaven and on earth and under the earth." He first came as a humble baby and Suffering Servant, but when He returns, it is as the Conquering King. But do you treat Him that way? Perhaps you know that to accept Jesus as your Savior you must "confess with your mouth Jesus as Lord" (Romans 10:9), but do you acknowledge His authority with your life? Do you address Him with the respect He deserves?

I believe we are provided with an excellent illustration of the reverence we are to demonstrate toward Christ through the account in Scripture of the wise men from the East who went to see Jesus. If you recall, those men left everything behind to seek and know Him. They said, "Where is He who has been born King of the Jews? For we saw His star in the east and have come to worship Him" (Matthew 2:2). These magi were influential counselors and astronomers, probably from somewhere in Mesopotamia. Perhaps they were descendants of those who learned from the prophet Daniel when he lived in Babylon. Daniel, who rose to prominence

Worship is the reaction that
comes from recognizing the
Lord's overwhelming love,
mercy, and grace toward us.

among the advisors of the Babylonian and Medo–Persian empires, taught that the Jews expected a Messiah who would set them free. Generations later, when the sign of the Jewish King appeared in the sky, those wise men understood its significance and took action.

These magi serve as a good example for us because their hearts were set on worshiping the coming King. Worship is the conscious—though often spontaneous—reaction that comes from experiencing and recognizing the Lord's overwhelming love, mercy, and grace toward us. We are in awe of who God is— the Sovereign of the universe, who has compassionately chosen to be our intimate and loving Redeemer, Provider, Protector, Healer, Leader, and Friend. We exalt Him because of His incalculable worth, His glory, His holiness, and His extraordinary kindness to us—attributing to Him the eternal, magnificent praise that exclusively and eternally belong to Him.

As such, the wise men worshiped Christ by unfailingly watching for His appearing. Second, when they saw the signs that He had come, they immediately left everything behind, searched diligently for Him, and did not stop until they could draw near to Him. Third, they exalted Jesus by telling others about Him. Fourth, they rejoiced at His presence and laid their treasures at His feet.

The wise men's actions parallel how we are to live as believers. After all, Jesus taught us, "You must worship the LORD your God and serve only him" (Luke 4:8 NLT). And like the magi, we are called to *watch faithfully*. We are to fix "our eyes on Jesus, the author and perfecter of faith" (Hebrews 12:2). We are to study Scripture with the goal of knowing Jesus, serving Him, and recognizing the signs of His return. And as we watch, we are to wait patiently for Him.

Second, we are to *work diligently*—leaving behind whatever hinders us, strengthening our relationship with Jesus and continually drawing nearer to Him. We should actively seek to follow His will for our lives and serve the Lord with the gifts and resources He has provided to us.

Third, we are to *witness intentionally*. We should be telling others about the love of God and the good news of salvation through Jesus Christ. We are to testify about what the Lord has done in our lives, both through word and by our example. We are also to help others grow spiritually, developing an ever-increasing intimacy with and devotion to Christ.

Finally, in all these things, we are to *worship Jesus wholeheartedly*—rejoicing in Him and laying our treasures at His feet. We exalt Him with everything we have and everything we are because of who He is.

Friend, Jesus is coming back as the reigning, victorious King. This means that, ultimately, we will triumph in every situation and circumstance. Therefore, we do not have to be anxious about bad news. No matter what happens on this earth, we can take comfort in knowing that we have eternal life and serve the One who is always victorious.

However, recognizing the lordship of Christ and anticipating His imminent return should also change how we live. When we believe Jesus could come back any moment, we are likely to be

Jesus is coming back as the reigning, victorious King.

more careful about how we operate and more motivated to serve Him. We are also more conscious of our influence on our friends and loved ones who may not believe in Christ. We do not know how much time we have to tell them about the greatest gift we have ever been given, so we realize we must make the most of every opportunity to show them Jesus' love.

Jesus said, "I am coming quickly, and My reward is with Me, to render to every man according to what he has done" (Revelation 22:12). Therefore, we cannot take the days, weeks, months, or years we are given for granted. We know Jesus has prepared a place for us in heaven, along with blessings and rewards for the way we've faithfully served Him in this life. So let Christmas remind you to keep your returning King as your focus and worship Jesus with your life. Because ultimately, my friend, that is the path to life at its very best—in this world and in the one to come.

A Moment of Reflection

Write out Revelation 16:15:

_____

_____

_____

_____

_____

If Jesus were to come back today, what aspects of your life would you wish were different before Him? How do you want to change your life before He returns?

_____

_____

_____

_____

_____

_____

_____

_____

_____

_____

Spend time asking God to help you live a life that is pleasing to Him. As He shows you what to do, agree with Him in prayer.

_____

_____

_____

_____

_____

_____

_____

_____

_____

_____

Spend time worshiping Jesus as your returning and conquering King!

_____

_____

_____

_____

_____

_____

_____

_____

_____

_____

_____

_____

_____

A Gift for Today

Do you want your life to count for eternity? Do you want to hear "Well done, faithful servant" when you see Jesus face-to-face?

You can make every moment of your life worthwhile and pleasing to Jesus by worshiping God, obeying Him, and loving others in His name.

The advent of our King
Our prayers must now employ,
And we must hymns of welcome sing
In strains of holy joy.
The everlasting Son
Incarnate deigns to be;
Himself a servant's form puts on
To set His servants free . . .
As Judge, on clouds of light,
He soon will come again
And His true members all unite
With Him in heaven to reign.
Before the dawning day
Let sin's dark deeds be gone,
The old man all be put away,
The new man now put on.
All glory to the Son,
Who comes to set us free,
With Father, Spirit, ever One,
Through all eternity.
"THE ADVENT OF OUR KING" BY CHARLES COFFIN[13]

NOTES

1. William Henry Monk, *Hymns Ancient and Modern* (New York: Pott & Amery, 1870), 39, verses 1, 5–6, "Of the Father's Love Begotten," The Hymns and Carols of Christmas, accessed March 4, 2022, https://www.hymnsandcarolsofchristmas.com/Hymns_and_Carols/of_the_fathers_love_begotten-1.htm.

2. "Hark! The Herald Angels Sing," original lyrics by Charles Wesley, hymnal.net, accessed March 4, 2022, https://www.hymnal.net/en/hymn/h/84.

3. "Veni, Veni, Emmanuel," originally in *Psalteriolum Cantionum Catholicarum* (1710), Choral Public Domain Library, updated July 4, 2021, https://www.cpdl.org/wiki/index.php/O_come,_O_come_Emmanuel.

4. Spiros Zodhiates, *The Complete Word Study New Testament* (Chattanooga, TN: AMG Publishers, 1992), 1471–1472, and Gerhard Kittel, G. W. Bromiley, Gerhard Friedrich, and Ronald E. Pitkin, *Theological Dictionary of the New Testament* Vol. 9 (Grand Rapids, MI: Wm. B. Eerdmans Publishing Company, 1964), 372–402.

5. William Henry Husk, *Songs of the Nativity* (London: John Camden Hotten, 1868), 56–58, https://ia800208.us.archive.org/13/items/cu31924073426169/cu31924073426169.pdf.

6. *A Selection of Hymns* (Dublin: RM Tims, 1830), 8, https://tinyurl.com/32fe5934.

7. Monk, *Hymns Ancient and Modern*, 38.

8. "Angels, from the Realms of Glory" HymnTime.com, updated February 11, 2022, by James Montgomery, http://www.hymntime.com/tch/htm/a/f/r/g/afrglory.htm.

9. Husk, *Songs of the Nativity*, 70–73.

10. Charles Wesley, "Come, Thou Long-Expected Jesus," Hymnary.org, accessed March 4, 2022, https://hymnary.org/text/come_thou_long_expected_jesus_born_to.

11. John Morrison, "To Us a Child of Hope Is Born," The Hymns and Carols of Christmas, accessed March 4, 2022, https://www.hymnsandcarolsofchristmas.com/Hymns_and_Carols/to_us_a_child_of_hope_is_born.htm.

12. Henry Van Dyke, "The Hymn of Joy," in The Poems of Henry Van Dyke (New York: Scribner's Sons, 1912), 332, https://www.google.com/books/edition/The_Poems_of_Henry_Van_Dyke/w0xAAQAAMAAJ.

13. Charles Coffin, "The Advent of Our King," trans. John Chandler, Christian Classics Ethereal Library, accessed March 4, 2022, https://www.ccel.org/ccel/anonymous/luth_hymnal/tlh068.htm.

ABOUT THE AUTHOR

D r. Charles Stanley is the pastor emeritus of the First Baptist Church of Atlanta, where he has served for more than 50 years. He is a *New York Times* bestselling author who has written more than 70 books, including the bestselling devotional *Every Day in His Presence*. Dr. Stanley is the founder of In Touch Ministries. The *In Touch with Dr. Charles Stanley* program is transmitted on more than 4,000 television, radio, and satellite networks and stations worldwide, in more than 75 heart languages. The award-winning *In Touch* devotional magazine is printed in four languages and sent to more than one million subscribers monthly. Dr. Stanley's goal is best represented by Acts 20:24: "Life is worth nothing unless I use it for doing the work assigned me by the Lord Jesus—the work of telling others the Good News about God's mighty kindness and love." This is because, as he says, "It is the Word of God and the work of God that changes people's lives."